100
WISDOM

ARCTURUS

To Kelah

With our best
wishes on your
18th birthday!
Love
The Labontés

With special thanks to Anne Moreland

ARCTURUS

This edition published in 2013 by Arcturus Publishing Limited
26/27 Bickels Yard, 151–153 Bermondsey Street,
London SE1 3HA

ISBN: 978-1-84858-547-8
AD002186EN

Printed in China

Contents

Introduction

Throughout our lives, we seek wisdom – the knowledge of how to understand and act for the best. As we get older, we hope to use our intelligence and experience to help us deal with the problems we encounter. Sometimes we fail; sometimes we succeed.

But whatever happens, we know we must keep learning, whether from others or from ourselves. This little book will help you to do that, by offering you a store of wisdom to dip into, ranging from the profound to the comical, and collected from many different cultures over the centuries. It can't guarantee to make you wise, but it will make you think, and hopefully help you on your way.

What is
Wisdom?

Wisdom is more than just knowledge; it also involves judgement, experience and intelligence, as well as empathy and other qualities. How do we gain it; why do we need it; and when do we use it?

It is not knowledge that makes us wise,
but understanding how to use it.

Many come to wisdom
through failure, rather
than success.

We become wise only when we learn
to regard all human beings as equal.
There can be no wisdom in prejudice.

The candle of love burns out quickly, but the flame of wisdom burns forever.

From listening comes wisdom, from speaking, regret.

Knowledge is the best remedy for fear.

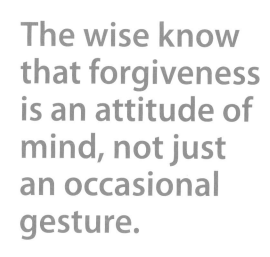

The wise know that forgiveness is an attitude of mind, not just an occasional gesture.

Reason governs the wise man,
and cudgels the fool.

Trouble brings experience and experience brings wisdom.

Wisdom is about looking outward, as well as looking inward; And looking forward, as well as looking back.

The wise person knows that no answer is a kind of answer.

We will be known forever by the tracks we leave.

Native American proverb

Fools rush in where angels fear to tread.

Be kind whenever possible.
More often, we regret having been
unkind than having been too kind.

A poet begins in delight and ends in wisdom.
Robert Frost

No one ever solved a problem at four o'clock in the morning. Better to go back to sleep and wake up with a clear head. In daylight, your sense of proportion will return.

There is no greater sorrow than knowing everything, because we humans live for questions.

Wisdom is not the same as knowledge. A person may know a lot, but be a fool. In the same way, a simple man may be profoundly wise.

If it ain't broke, don't fix it!

Age doesn't always bring wisdom.
Sometimes age comes all by itself.

Know yourself better than those who speak of you.

Knowledge cuts up the world.
Wisdom makes it whole.

Brazilian proverb

Not to know is bad. Not to wish to know is worse...

Humility and knowledge breed wisdom.

Knowledge comes, but wisdom lingers.
Alfred, Lord Tennyson

There is wisdom in knowing what you need to know, and being wise enough to keep it to yourself.

Knowledge is knowing that the street is one way. Wisdom is looking in both directions all the same.

Wise men say nothing in dangerous times.

Aesop

Wisdom is a deep understanding of people, events, and situations. It requires, first and foremost, control of one's emotional reactions so that reason and knowledge, not passion, determine one's actions.

Procrastination is the thief of time.

Wisdom is knowing what is right, and being able to act upon that knowledge.

No one can be wise at all times, and even the wisest person is subject to foolishness.

Be wise; make the best use of what you know, and what you can do with what you know.

Philosophy, according to the Greeks, is the love of wisdom.

Wisdom is knowing *why* things are a certain way, not just that things *are* a certain way.

Of all the virtues, wisdom is the greatest.

Be wiser than other people if you can, but do not tell them so.

The fool wonders, the wise man asks.

Benjamin Disraeli

Confess you were wrong yesterday; it will show you are wise today.

A wise person can see what needs to be done, and can do it successfully without being told how to go about it.

**The wise propose,
but fools determine.**

A rich child often
sits in a poor
mother's lap.

Before you can hope to be wise you must start at the beginning, and learn to see things as they truly are.

Footprints on the sands of time are not made by sitting down.

He who is slow to anger has great wisdom.
He who has a quick temper exalts folly.
The Bible

Wisdom is the capacity to realize what is of value in life, for oneself and others, and pursue it.

Try and trust will move mountains.

Wisdom is the co-ordination of knowledge and experience, and its deliberate use to improve wellbeing.

You will know when you come upon a wise woman, because others will go to her for advice.

Wisdom is the greatest gift of humankind.

A wise man never speaks his wisdom unless he is asked to do so.

33

The best mirror is an old friend.

Knowing others is intelligence.
Knowing yourself is true wisdom.
Mastering others is strength.
Mastering yourself is true power.
Tao Te Ching

Listen to those who speak little. It may be that they know most.

The man who is free from hatred and fear is wise.

Words are potent weapons for all causes, good or bad.

The wisdom of hindsight is of no use whatsoever. *Indian proverb*

One can judge the real character of a man by the way he treats those who can do nothing for him.

It's tough trying to keep your feet on the ground, your head above the clouds, your nose to the grindstone, your shoulder to the wheel, your finger on the pulse, your eye on the ball, and your ear to the ground.

Ignorance is the night of the mind,
but a night without moon or star.
Confucius

Rebuke with soft words and hard arguments.

Young people talk of what they are doing; the old, of what they have done; and fools, of what they want to do.

Talking without thinking is like shooting without taking aim.

Riches serve a wise man but command a fool.

To act according to the moment is the best wisdom I know. *Horace Walpole*

A wise man changes his mind frequently, while a fool stands fast, come what may.

Nothing good ever ends.

Wisdom is not wisdom unless it has come through making mistakes.

Those who are wise forever seek wisdom; those who are foolish believe they have found it.

Before you can score, you must first have a goal.

**Don't walk behind me
I may not lead
Don't walk in front of me
I may not follow
Walk beside me
That we may be as one.**

Native American proverb

Want of wisdom is more to be pitied
than want of possessions.

No man is born wise. Wisdom cannot be learned, for it is a journey of discovery where the destination remains unknown.

To know when you have enough is to be rich indeed.

Wisdom is like the darkness. In darkness, all colours can agree.

It is better to be sometimes cheated than never to trust.

Morality is understanding that others should be treated the way you yourself would wish to be treated.

We constantly make mistakes when we are trying to be wise. But if we stop trying to be wise, we stop knowing that we're making mistakes.

The path of wisdom is steep and stony;
it takes courage to set out upon it.

Conduct yourself
in such a way that
you bring joy to
your friends, and
none to your foes.

The wise person is sometimes content to play the fool.

Each day, when we awake, we are reborn. We have a new chance to make a fresh start.

Wisdom consists in knowing when to speak, and when to hold one's peace.

Don't approach a goat from the front, a horse from the back, or a fool from any side. *Jewish proverb*

It is useless to quarrel over religion. All great religions seek the same goal, which is spiritual enlightenment; they simply choose different paths to get there.

A fool may talk; a wise man speaks.

Wisdom lends the highest authority to action.

Without wisdom, wealth is worthless.

Walk lightly in the spring
Mother earth is about to give birth.
Native American proverb

Be satisfied with needs, not wants.

Genius is distinct from wisdom.
Genius is a gift, while wisdom is
a craft that we must learn.

Wise men see and hear as little children
do. *Lao Tzu*

**The biggest fool is the person
who boasts of their wisdom.**

For the wise, learning never ends.

To resolve a problem, we must first admit that we may have been wrong.

The paradox of the wise is that they know they are not wise.

The wise person must have many types of knowledge. To know what the goal of life is; to assess whether that goal is achievable; to find out how to reach it; how to avoid danger; how to take advantage of opportunity; how to understand others, and oneself; how to endure the difficulties of life; and last, but not least, how to savour its joys.

A Short Course in Human Relations:
The six most important words:
   I admit that I was wrong
The five most important words:
   You did a great job
The four most important words:
   What do you think?
The three most important words:
   Could you please…?
The two most important words:
   Thank you
The most important word: 'we'
 The least important word: 'I'

Wisdom is: acceptance; gratitude; attentiveness; kindness; patience; commitment; wonder; insight; empathy; respect; integrity; joy; intelligence; courage; equanimity; co-operation; serenity; honesty; curiosity; openness; and many other qualities.

All things by immortal power are
To one another joined
So that one cannot disturb a flower
Without the troubling of a star.

Francis Thompson

Adversity makes a person wise, but not rich.

Science gives us knowledge, but only philosophy gives us wisdom. *Will Durant*

A teacher sees tomorrow in a child's eye.

Don't argue with an idiot; people watching may not be able to tell the difference!

Making others feel better generally makes us feel better; and making others feel worse generally makes us feel worse.

The secret of being wise is to know how to give meaning to life's dull routines.

Enjoy the little things in life; one day you may look back and realize they were the big things.

Whoever in this world overcomes their selfish cravings, their sorrows fall away, like drops of water from a lotus flower.
Dhammapada

Wisdom is a life that knows it's worth living.

Youth is a gift of nature; age is a work of art.

Wisdom travels from your head to your heart to your hands.

When it comes to the future, there are three kinds of people: those who let it happen, those who make it happen, and those who wonder what happened. Most of us are in the last category!

Time ripens all things; no person is born wise. *Cervantes*

The Path to Wisdom

Gaining wisdom may well be a goal in itself, but more often it simply accrues as we travel along life's path. Being aware of the pitfalls, as well as the pleasures, of the journey, and knowing how to cope with them, is part of our task as human beings, and one that we do well to reflect upon.

It's not the hand you're dealt in life that counts; it's how you play your cards.

Sometimes, it's worth asking yourself: if I could have anything I wanted in life, what would it be? You may find that the things that really matter, you already have.

Don't try to predict the future; instead, try to invent it.

If you worry about what people think of you, bear in mind that most of the time, people will not be thinking about you. They will be thinking about themselves.

Enthusiasm is one of the most precious gifts in life. Everyone is born with it, but as we grow up, we begin to lose it. The trick is to hold on to as much of it as possible – even if it means being a little childish at times!

If money can solve a problem, then it's not a serious problem.

Our birth is but a sleep and a forgetting
The soul that rises with us, our life's star,
Hath elsewhere had its setting
And cometh from afar. *William Wordsworth*

The beginning of wisdom is experience.

Your own soul is nourished when you are kind; it is destroyed when you are cruel. *King Solomon*

Fame and fortune should serve a purpose; they are not an end in themselves.

Sometimes the wicked prosper, and the good are unlucky. This is a fact of life that the wise understand, and the foolish cannot accept.

On your way up, treat those you meet with kindness and courtesy; you are sure to meet them again on your way down.

Remember, it ain't over till it's over.

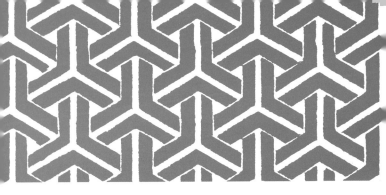

None of us can accept that we are really quite ordinary; that is because, in a sense, none of us are. For we are all, each and every one of us, quite unique.

There's no such thing as a free lunch.

I have come into the world to see this:
The sword drops from mens' hands
Even at the height of their arc of rage
Because we have finally realized
There is just one flesh we can wound.
Hafiz

We cannot always predict the future; but we can experience, and learn from, the present.

Sometimes it's hard to see the wood for the trees. Don't focus entirely on the small tasks you must do every day; instead, look up, and see where they are taking you.

If you try to do the impossible, you may find you reach the limit of the possible.

In life, we must face the fact that, however hard we try, we may not achieve our goals. That is a possibility. But if we don't try, we are certain not to achieve our goals!

Sometimes we solve a problem and reach a conclusion. More often, we just reach a conclusion because we're bored of thinking about a problem.

You can't have your cake and eat it. Obvious perhaps, but it's surprising how many people try to.

Do as you would be done by.

We shall not cease from exploration
And the end of all our exploring will be to
Arrive where we started
And to know the place for the first time.
T.S. Eliot

Wise people are those who are able to admit, from time to time, that they are wrong.

If you hate someone, or feel patronized by them, you are allowing them to have some kind of hold over you. Don't let them wind you up!

All's fair in love and war.

Calmness; balance; courage; optimism; kindness; confidence; slowness to anger; the ability to laugh at life's uncertainties. These are the qualities of the wise man or woman.

The golden rule is that there is no golden rule.

George Bernard Shaw

Is your cup of care full to the brim? Empty it from time to time, before you start to fill it up again.

Wisdom is a combination of experience, knowledge, and understanding. It's also tolerance, to cope with the ups and downs of life, and awareness of how events will play out over the long term.

Intelligence is a necessary but not sufficient condition of wisdom.

When you're walking along, can you see what's ahead? Or are you too busy looking down at your feet?

Those who would be constant in happiness or wisdom must change often.
Confucius

A health scare can remind you what's important about life, and encourage you to think more carefully about how you want to live in the future.

To the world, you may be one person. But to one person, you may be the world.

A wise old owl lived in an oak
The more he saw, the less he spoke
The less he spoke, the more he heard
Why aren't we like that wise old bird?

The art of living well lies in paying attention to detail, but not letting yourself get bogged down by it.

Clouds come floating into my life, no longer to carry rain or usher storm, but to add colour to my sunset sky.
Rabindranath Tagore

Wisdom: knowledge of what is true or right, as well as good judgement as to what to do about it.

In life, each of us must sometimes play the fool.

Spend less time brooding about the past. Let go of old grudges, resentments, worries. Instead, think about the possibilities ahead of you.

Once in a while, plan a day when you make no plans at all…

**In the depth of winter
I finally learned
That there was in me
an invincible summer.**

Albert Camus

The best way to knock the chip
off your neighbour's shoulder is
to pat him on the back.

Those who wish to sing will always find a song.

If you are wise, you can accommodate yourself to all the many contingencies of life; if you are a fool, you will struggle against them, like a swimmer against the tide.

**A person consists of his faith.
Whatever his faith is, so is he.**

Our worst experiences can sometimes make our funniest memories.

It's so simple to be wise. Just think of something stupid to say, and then don't say it.
Sam Levenson

Tell your friend a lie; if he keeps it a secret, tell him the truth.

Wisdom: sagacity, discernment, and insight.

When you get angry, recognize that you are so. Take a deep breath, count to ten, and only after you've done that, decide what you are going to say or do.

One should go invited to a friend in good fortune; and uninvited in misfortune.
Swedish proverb

We must take change by the hand, or rest assuredly, change will take us by the throat.

Winston Churchill

Sometimes a piece of bad luck can turn out to be a golden opportunity for change.

The best parents are those who can let their children be the people they are, instead of deciding who they are for them.

It is important to have aims in life. But it's also important to be open to change, and to see the positive when circumstances conspire to make our goals impossible.

Do not erase the present by thinking about the future.

Looking inside ourselves, to discover our true thoughts and feelings, is an important step on the path to wisdom. But we must make sure to look outside ourselves, at the world and at our fellow human beings, as well.

Experience tells us that, once we escape one misfortune in our lives, we soon find another to worry about.

Pursue wealth, not money; they are two different things.

If you could speak to your younger self, what advice would you give him or her? The more mistakes you've made, the better your advice will be.

Live in harmony with yourself, and you will live in harmony with others.

The wise person listens carefully when others speak, holding back the impulse to respond, interrupt, or give an opinion until it is asked for.

Mortals grow swiftly in misfortune. *Hesiod*

The wealthiest man in the world is he who has good health throughout his life.

We often feel more affection for those who are enduring suffering than for those who are having great success in life.

The man who never alters his opinions is like standing water, and breeds reptiles of the mind. *William Blake*

Listen to the voice of conscience; it will usually be worth listening to.

Fools know that they know; the wise know that they don't.

If you can't understand an individual, try looking at the situation from his or her point of view. You will be surprised how different it looks to them.

Here is the rule to remember in the future. When anything tempts you to be bitter: not 'This is a misfortune', but 'To bear this worthily is good fortune'.
Marcus Aurelius

Sometimes the wisest remarks come from the mouths of little children.

If you look back at your past, you are bound to find many lessons in it for the future.

The greatest strength is gentleness.

Native American proverb

When you wake up after a dream, don't immediately dismiss it as nonsense. Think about it. Ask yourself, what could this be trying to tell me? Listen to your dreams; they may be sending you a message.

You will never be able to come up with an idea all by yourself. Each and every one of us learns from those who have gone before.

True wisdom cannot be measured in terms of what the world thinks. Sometimes a wise decision can look like a foolish one at the time.

Flex your wisdom muscle; like your body, your mind needs exercise.

Humankind has not woven the web of life. We are but one thread within it. Whatever we do to the web, we do to ourselves. *Chief Seattle*

Most of us want the things that money can buy; but once our basic needs are satisfied, the things that make us happiest are the things money *can't* buy.

The wise person makes sure
not to have too many opinions,
especially on subjects he knows
nothing about.

I love those who can smile in trouble, who can gather strength from distress, and grow brave by reflection. 'Tis the business of little minds to shrink, but they whose heart is firm, and whose conscience approves their conduct, will pursue their principles unto death. *Leonardo da Vinci*

Wisdom doesn't necessarily come with age. Sometimes all we get as we grow older is wrinkles.

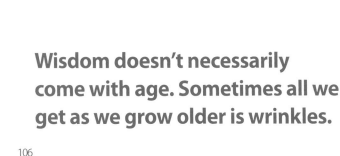

Firelight won't let you read fine stories, but it's warm and you won't see the dust on the floor. *Irish proverb*

I have been to the end of the earth.
I have been to the end of the water.
I have been to the end of the sky.
I have been to the end of the mountains.
I have found none that are not my friends.

Navajo poem

When we are young, days seem long.
As we grow older, and begin to look back,
they start to get shorter and shorter.

Failure is sometimes the first step on the path to success.

The perfect man uses his mind as a mirror. It grasps nothing, it rejects nothing. It receives but does not keep. *Chuang Tzu*

Just as calm comes after the storm, out of turmoil and conflict can come peace and tranquillity.

It's easy to give advice, but hard to take it.

A man wrapped up in himself makes a very small parcel.

John Ruskin

If we expect material possessions to make us happy we are bound to be disappointed.

Eat food. Not too much. Mostly plants.

Michael Pollan

The past is the past;
we can learn from
it, but we should
not grieve for it,
since we cannot
change it.

Silence has more meaning than noise.

If you are wise, you will value your friends, and make sure to keep them throughout your life.

A fool sees not the same tree that a wise man sees.

William Blake

How is it that, through difficulty, some people achieve deep understanding and wisdom, while others simply despair?

Valuing the good things of life – family, friends, health, and purposeful activity – is one of the cornerstones of true wisdom.

It is not the strongest of the species that survive, nor the most intelligent, but the one most responsive to change.
Charles Darwin

Trying to master a skill
can be a long, painstaking
business that requires
not only patience, but the
wisdom to understand
that perfection can never
be achieved.

**If we want to live life to the full, we
must take risks. Without sorrow,
there is no joy; without loss, no
gain; without conflict, no peace.**

Money is like gasoline during a road trip. You don't want to run out of gas on your trip, but you're not doing a tour of gas stations.

Tim O'Reilly

Recognizing how you yourself learn is the key to turning experience into wisdom.

It is pleasant when those around you agree with you; but you may find you learn more about yourself, and the world, when they don't.

Knowledge based on experience allows you to adapt your behaviour. Wisdom is a combination of reasoning, judgement, and the ability to appreciate the long-term consequences of that behaviour.

I long to accomplish a great and noble task; but my chief duty is to accomplish small tasks as if they were great and noble.
Helen Keller

Wisdom lies not in trying to be somebody, but in trying to help somebody.

If you think you are not conceited, it means you are very conceited indeed. *C.S. Lewis*

We learn to be wise by making mistakes.

Wisdom is the ability to stay calm in a crisis, and to deal with life's difficulties through common sense and sound judgement. Yet it is more than this: it is also an understanding of life's mysteries, and a deep insight into the workings of the human mind.

If every fool wore a crown, we'd all be kings. *Welsh proverb*

When pride cometh, then cometh shame; but with the lowly is wisdom. ***The Bible***

Sometimes it's best to remain silent, even when you know you are right. In time, others will come to realize what you already know.

Don't let your triumphs go to your head, or your failures go to your heart.

The fool waits for something wonderful to happen; the wise man finds wonder in the everyday.

No mention shall be made of coral, or of pearls. For the price of wisdom is above rubies.
The Bible

After the dark of the night comes the daylight of wisdom.

Wisdom cannot exist without reflection, compassion, tolerance, kindness, forgiveness, patience, humility, and most of all, love.

When someone starts a remark by saying 'With respect', you can be sure they're going to say something disrespectful!

A good laugh and a long sleep are the best cures in the doctor's book.

Do not be afraid to be sad. By so doing, you may free your mind of sad thoughts, and become joyful again.

No one can instruct you in the ways of wisdom; it is a secret that you must learn for yourself.

Once you have gone through a difficult experience and survived, you will gain confidence. For you will know that next time trouble comes your way, you will be able to deal with it.

What soap is to the body, laughter is to the soul. *Yiddish proverb*

Solitude is not the same as loneliness.
It may provide us with a chance to think,
work, and rest without distraction. It
is an essential part of our spiritual and
creative lives, and one that we need to
pay attention to from time to time.

Wise Sayings

There have been many wise religious leaders, philosophers, anonymous thinkers, artists, and poets who have sought to pass on the fruit of their experience. Some of them have achieved wisdom through success; others through failure, which, as it turns out, teaches us just as much about ourselves and the world around us.

What is it to be wise?

'Tis but to know how little can be known

To see all other's faults, and feel our own.

Alexander Pope

Science is organized knowledge. Wisdom is organized life.

Immanuel Kant

The beginning of wisdom is found in doubting; by doubting we come to the question, and by seeking we may come upon the truth.

Pierre Abelard

The doors of wisdom are never shut.

Benjamin Franklin

**Before you can be old and wise,
you must first be young and stupid.**

Believe those who are seeking
the truth; doubt those who find it.
André Gide

A word to the wise ain't necessary; it's the stupid ones who need the advice.

Bill Cosby

If man will begin with certainties, he shall end in doubts; but if he will be content to begin with doubts, he shall end in certainties. *Francis Bacon*

Each morning sees some task begun
Each evening sees it close
Something attempted, something done
Has earned a night's repose.
Henry Wadsworth Longfellow

The art of being wise is the art of knowing what to overlook.

William James

The best way to avoid a bad action is by doing a good one. *John Clare*

A stumble may prevent a fall. *Thomas Fuller*

You can tell whether a man is clever by his answers. You can tell whether a man is wise by his questions.
Naguib Mahfouz

Wisdom begins at the end.
Daniel Webster

Thinking is easy but acting is difficult, and to put one's thoughts into action is the most difficult thing in the world.

Johann Wolfgang von Goethe

Some folks are wise, and some are otherwise.

Tobias Smollett

The reasonable man adapts himself to the world; the unreasonable one persists in trying to adapt the world to himself. Therefore, all progress depends on the unreasonable man.

George Bernard Shaw

When an argument flares up, the wise man quenches it by silence.

They whom truth and wisdom lead
Can gather honey from a weed.
William Cowper

Be happy. It is one way of being wise.
Colette

Life is what happens to you when you're busy making other plans. *John Lennon*

Human felicity is produced not so much by great pieces of good fortune that seldom happen, as by little advantages that occur every day.

Benjamin Franklin

**What do I think of Western civilization?
I think it would be a very good idea.**
Mohandas Gandhi

Almost every wise saying
has an opposite, no less
wise, to balance it.

George Santayana

A loving heart is the truest wisdom.
Charles Dickens

Besides the noble art of getting
things done, there is the noble
art of leaving things undone.
The wisdom of life consists in
the elimination of non-essentials.
Yutang Lin

A mistake is simply another way of doing things.

Katharine Graham

The man of wisdom is never of two minds;
The man of benevolence never worries;
The man of courage is never afraid.
Confucius

The invariable mark of wisdom is to see the miraculous in the common.

Ralph Waldo Emerson

Wisdom is ofttimes nearer when we stoop than when we soar.

William Wordsworth

Patience is the companion of wisdom.

Saint Augustine

Common sense in an uncommon degree is what the world calls wisdom.
Samuel Taylor Coleridge

Learning sleeps and snores in libraries, but wisdom is everywhere, wide awake, on tiptoe. *Josh Billings*

The fool doth think he is wise, but the wise man knows himself to be a fool.

William Shakespeare

The Lord prefers common-looking people.
That is why he makes so many of them.
Abraham Lincoln

Science investigates, religion interprets. Science gives man knowledge, which is power. Religion gives man wisdom, which is control. Science deals mainly with facts, religion mainly with values. The two are not rivals.

Martin Luther King

A man begins cutting his wisdom teeth the first time he bites off more than he can chew.

Herb Caen

Years teach us more than books.

Berthold Auerbach

The only medicine for the suffering, crime, and all the other woes of mankind, is wisdom.

Thomas Huxley

The seat of knowledge is in the head; of wisdom, in the heart. We are sure to judge wrong, if we do not feel right.

William Hazlitt

Not to know at large of things remote
From use, obscure and subtle, but to know
That which before us lies in daily life
Is the prime wisdom. *John Milton*

No one can make you feel inferior without your consent.

Eleanor Roosevelt

One must not lose faith in humanity;
humanity is an ocean; if a few drops
of the ocean are dirty, the ocean does
not become dirty.

Mohandas Gandhi

**If you speak softly and carry a
big stick, you will go far.**

Theodore Roosevelt

Pick battles big enough to matter, small enough to win.

Jonathan Kozol

There is an element of truth in every idea that lasts long enough to be called corny.
Irving Berlin

The greatest lesson in life is to know that even fools are right sometimes.

Winston Churchill

Nothing in life is to be feared. It is only to be understood. Now is the time to understand more so that we may fear less.

Marie Curie

No problem can withstand the assault of sustained thinking. ***Voltaire***

To be angry is to revenge the faults of others on ourselves. *Alexander Pope*

Knowledge is proud that he has learned so much Wisdom is humble that he knows no more. *William Cowper*

Mistakes are the portals of discovery.

James Joyce

What does not destroy me, makes me stronger.
Friedrich Nietzsche

Learn wisdom from the ways of a seedling. A seedling which is never hardened off through stressful situations will never become a strong, productive plant.

Stephen Sigmund

It is a common experience that a problem difficult at night is resolved in the morning after the committee of sleep has worked on it.

John Steinbeck

Opinions have caused more ills than the plague and earthquakes on this little globe of ours.

Voltaire

Books give wisdom where none was before But where some is, their reading makes it more.

John Harington

Honesty is the first chapter of the book of wisdom. *Thomas Jefferson*

Man can embody truth but he cannot know it. *W.B. Yeats*

Four things support the world: the learning of the wise, the justice of the great, the prayers of the good, and the valour of the brave.

Muhammad

Keep me away from the wisdom that does not cry, the philosophy that does not laugh, and the greatness that does not bow before children.

Khalil Gibran

I have always thought the actions of men are the best interpreters of their thoughts.
John Locke

The ink of the scholar is more sacred than the blood of the martyr.
Muhammad

Humankind cannot bear very much reality.

T.S. Eliot

What is tolerance? It is the consequence of humanity. We are all formed of frailty and error; let us pardon reciprocally each other's folly – that is the first law of nature.

Voltaire

One's first step in wisdom is to question everything – and one's last to come to terms with everything.

George C. Lichtenberg

A prudent question is one half of wisdom.

Francis Bacon

Early to bed and early to rise
Makes a man healthy, wealthy, and wise.
Benjamin Franklin

Anger is a wind that blows out the lamp of the mind.

Robert G. Ingersoll

Human beings are members of a whole
In creation of one essence and soul.
If you have no sympathy for human pain
The name of human you cannot retain.
Saadi

Only those who dare to fail greatly can ever achieve greatly.

Robert F. Kennedy

Your vision will become clear only when you look into your heart… Who looks outside, dreams. Who looks inside, awakens. *Carl Jung*

The more a man judges, the less he loves.

Honoré de Balzac

There are no passengers on Spaceship Earth. We are all crew.

Marshall McLuhan

The teacher who is indeed wise does not bid you to enter the house of his wisdom but rather leads you to the threshold of your mind.

Khalil Gibran

I'd rather regret the things I've done than the things I have not.
Lucille Ball

From the sublime to the ridiculous is but a step.

Napoléon Bonaparte

A single conversation with a wise man is better than ten years of study.

Chinese proverb

Show respect to all people and grovel to none.
When you arise in the morning, give thanks for
the food and for the joy of living.
If you see no reason for giving thanks, the fault
lies only in yourself.
Abuse no one and no thing, for abuse turns the
wise ones to fools and robs the spirit of its vision.

Tecumseh

Better be wise by the misfortunes of others than your own. *Aesop*

Water is fluid, soft, and yielding. But water will wear away rock, which is rigid and cannot yield. As a rule, whatever is fluid, soft, and yielding will overcome whatever is rigid and hard. This is another paradox; what is soft is strong. *Lao Tzu*

A wise man will make more opportunities than he finds.

Francis Bacon

He who lives without folly isn't as reasonable as he thinks.

François de la Rochefoucauld

The road of excess leads to the palace of wisdom; for we never know what is enough until we know what is more than enough.

William Blake

Wisdom is not a product of schooling but of the lifelong attempt to acquire it.

Albert Einstein

He's a fool who cannot conceal his wisdom.

Benjamin Franklin.

All human wisdom is summed up in two words: wait, and hope.

Alexandre Dumas

Knowledge speaks, but wisdom listens.
Jimi Hendrix

Make the most of yourself, for that is all there is to you. *Ralph Waldo Emerson*

As I slowly grow wise, I briskly grow cautious.

Mark Twain

Science gathers knowledge faster than society gathers wisdom.

Isaac Asimov

Holding on to anger is like grasping a hot coal with the intent of throwing it at someone else; you are the one who gets burned.

Buddha

Wisdom is founded on memory;
happiness on forgetfulness.
Mason Cooley

After wisdom comes wit.

Evan Esar

Wisdom is an inheritance which a wastrel cannot exhaust.

Karl Kraus

A man may be born to wealth, but wisdom comes only with length of days.

It requires wisdom to understand wisdom; the music is nothing if the audience is deaf.

Walter Lippmann

Doubt is the vestibule through which all must pass before they can enter into the temple of wisdom.
Charles Caleb Colton

Once all struggle is grasped, miracles are possible.

Mao Tse Tung

To learn moderation is the essence of sound sense and real wisdom.

Jacques-Bénigne Bossuet

The bird of wisdom flies low, and seeks her food under hedges; the eagle himself would be starved if he always soared aloft and against the sun.

Walter Savage Landor

If you want to make peace with your enemy, you have to work with your enemy. Then he becomes your partner. *Nelson Mandela*

The first sign of love is the last of wisdom. *Antoine Bret*

Every man feels instinctively that all the beautiful sentiments in the world weigh less than a single lovely action.

James Lowell

'Tis an old maxim in the schools
That flattery's the food of fools
Yet now and then your men of wit
Will condescend to take a bit.
Jonathan Swift

It requires a very unusual mind to undertake the analysis of the obvious. *Alfred North Whitehead*

When a man has not a good reason for doing a thing, he has one good reason for letting it alone.

Walter Scott

Man's main task is to give birth to himself.

Erich Fromm

A mountain is composed of tiny grains of earth. The ocean is made up of tiny drops of water. Even so, life is but an endless series of little details, actions, speeches, and thoughts. And the consequences, good or bad, of even the least of them are far- reaching. *Sivananda*

There is a road from the eye to the heart that does not go through the intellect.
G.K. Chesterton

The clouds may drop down titles and estates, and wealth may seek us, but wisdom must be sought. *Edward Young*

Health is the greatest gift, contentment the greatest wealth, faithfulness the best relationship.
Buddha

We don't receive wisdom; we must discover it for ourselves after a journey that no one can take for us or spare us. *Marcel Proust*

When a true genius appears, you can know him by this sign: that all the dunces are in a confederacy against him. *Jonathan Swift*

To live only for some future goal is shallow; it's the sides of the mountain that sustain life, not the top. *Robert M. Pirsig*

Where there is clarity and wisdom, there is neither fear nor ignorance. Where there is patience and humility, there is neither anger nor vexation. Where there is poverty and joy, there is neither greed nor avarice. Where there is peace and meditation, there is neither anxiety nor doubt. *Francis of Assisi*

Nothing difficult is ever easy.

A wise man asks himself the reason for his mistakes, while a fool will ask others.

This is what you shall do: love the earth and the sun and the animals, despise riches, give alms to everyone that asks, stand up for the stupid and crazy, devote your income and labour to others, hate tyrants, argue not concerning God …
Walt Whitman

When the sun rises, I go to work. When the sun goes down, I take my rest. I dig the well from which I drink. I farm the soil which yields my food. I share creation. Kings can do no more.

Chinese proverb

All children need a laptop. Not a computer, but a human laptop. Moms, Dads, Grannies and Grandpas, Aunts, Uncles – someone to hold them, read to them, teach them. **Colin Powell**

Mixing one's wines may be a mistake, but old and new wisdom mix admirably.

Bertolt Brecht

There is no wisdom save in truth. Truth is everlasting, but our ideas about truth are changeable. Only a little of the first fruits of wisdom, only a few fragments of the boundless heights, breadths and depths of truth, have I been able to gather. *Martin Luther*

The divine essence itself is love and wisdom. *Emanuel Swedenborg*

Solitude is the best nurse of wisdom.
Laurence Sterne

We can be knowledgeable with other men's knowledge, but we cannot be wise with other men's wisdom. *Michel de Montaigne*

The power is yours,
but not the sight;
You see not upon
what you tread;
You have the ages
for your guide,
But not the wisdom
to be led.

Edwin A. Robinson

The deed is everything; the glory is naught.

Johann Wolfgang von Goethe

What wisdom can you find that is greater than kindness?

Jean-Jacques Rousseau

Words of Wisdom

Many profess to be wise; the irony is that the wisest among us never do so, preferring instead to adopt a position of humility and compassion, in which the limits of human knowledge and experience are keenly felt. Here, we take a look at the mystery of the journey to wisdom, in which the more we find out, the less we realize that we know.

Wisdom consists in trying to bear in mind the true purpose of our lives; otherwise, it is all too easy to lose sight of what really counts.

Tout comprendre, c'est tout pardonner.
To understand all is to forgive all.

Let your imagination run free; but be wise enough to choose what is actually possible in reality.

The heart has its reasons, but reason does not always understand them.
Blaise Pascal

Confusion is part of life; we cannot avoid it. What we can do is to bring wisdom and insight to bear on difficult situations, whether or not we can change them.

Today is the tomorrow we worried about yesterday.

Worrying is like sitting in a rocking chair, tilting back and forth – it gives you something to do, but it doesn't get you anywhere.

The secret of health for both mind and body is not to mourn for the past, not to worry about the future, not to anticipate the future, but to live the present moment wisely and earnestly.
Buddha

If you can talk yourself into a state of anxiety and stress, you can talk yourself out of it, too.

What worries you, masters you.

John Locke

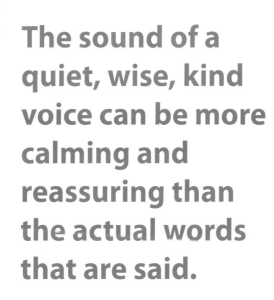

The sound of a quiet, wise, kind voice can be more calming and reassuring than the actual words that are said.

Justice, wisdom, and tolerance, are the building blocks of a fair society.

Without darkness there would be no light; without sadness, no joy.

Stop judging yourself. Banish the words, 'I should have'. Instead, start being as kind to yourself as you would be to a friend.

A genius is someone who aims at something no one else can see – and manages to hit the mark.

Wisdom gives its bearer natural authority, without the need for threats or promises.

Failure is the first page of the book of wisdom. Success the last.

Fear and superstition come out at night; in the morning, as the sun comes up, they go back to their hiding place.

Worry throws a big shadow over small things.

Swedish proverb

**I had a lot of tragedies in my life –
most of them never happened.**
Mark Twain

The ignorance of the young can be a kind of armour, shielding them from doubt and fear.

A little knowledge is a dangerous thing.

I hold it true, whate'er befall
I feel it when I sorrow most
'Tis better to have loved and lost
Than never to have loved at all.

Alfred Lord Tennyson

Just once in a while, we need to throw wisdom to the winds, and follow our hearts rather than our heads.

Being extremely busy can be a sign that you are not getting much done.

Happy the man who has broken the chains which hurt the mind, and has given up worrying once and for all. *Ovid*

Making plans and lists is important, but be careful that your plans and lists don't become a substitute for actually doing anything!

Courage is a beautiful kind of madness.

Life is an opportunity, benefit from it.
Life is a beauty, admire it.
Life is a dream, realize it.
Life is a challenge, meet it.
Life is a duty, complete it
Life is a game, play it.
Life is a promise, fulfil it.
Life is a song, sing it.
Life is a struggle, accept it.
Life is a tragedy, confront it.
Life is an adventure, dare it.
Life is luck, make it.
Life is life, fight for it! *Mother Teresa*

The wise person knows that it is, for the most part, impossible to comprehend or predict the behaviour of the human race.

Real wisdom lies in sincerity – the ability to show one's own feelings and speak truthfully, without fear of being thought foolish.

**Speak truth in humility to all people.
Only then can you be a true man.**

Native American proverb

One of the earliest lessons we learn
in life is that what hurts us, hurts
others. We cannot be wise if we
do not see that, in this respect, all
human beings are the same.

This above all: to thine own self be true
And it must follow, as the night the day,
Thou canst not then be false to any man.
William Shakespeare

It is natural to develop prejudices against people different from ourselves. It is noble to rise above them.

Indecision is itself a type of decision – to procrastinate.

Isn't it enough to see that a garden is beautiful, without believing that there are fairies at the bottom of it, too?

Douglas Adams

Art is a struggle between wisdom and madness.

If you fear the future, try thinking about what you *can* do about the situation, rather than focussing on what you *can't*.

Living according to your principles may lead you into adversity. That doesn't mean your principles are wrong, only that it's sometimes hard to stick by what you believe in.

There is no pillow so soft as a clear conscience.

The extreme limit of wisdom, that's what the public call madness.
Jean Cocteau

Your life may be the only book that others read.

Life may not be the party we were hoping for. But we can still dance.

Try to know wisdom, and likewise folly; but understand that expecting to be able to is like trying to catch the wind.

The miracle is not to fly through the air, or walk on water, but simply to walk the earth.

Chinese proverb

Too much of a good thing
can be wonderful. *Mae West*

**We tend to condemn in others
what we find in ourselves.**

We have, in fact, two kinds of morality side by side: one which we preach but do not practice, and another which we practice but seldom preach.
Bertrand Russell

Remember, you don't have to attend every argument you're invited to.

A man may smile and bid you hail
Yet wish you to the devil
But when a good dog wags his tail
You know he's on the level!

Conscience is what feels so, so bad when everything else feels so, so good.

The best way to succeed in life is to act on the advice we give to others.

There is no telling how far you will have to run if you chase your dreams.

Life is simple. But it isn't easy.

Too much sanity may be madness. And maddest of all, to see life as it is and not as it should be!

Miguel de Cervantes

We live and learn. Or not, as the case may be.

When the world says, 'Give up', Hope whispers, 'Try again, just one more time'.

It is right it should be so
Man was made for joy and woe
And when this we rightly know
Thro' the world we safely go.

Joy and woe are woven fine
A clothing for the soul divine
Under every grief and pine
Runs a joy with silken twine.

William Blake

Nobody trips over mountains. It's the small rocks and pebbles that cause you to stumble. If you can keep going in spite of these, you'll find that eventually, you'll have crossed the mountain.

Maybe that's what life is … a wink of the eye and winking stars.

Jack Kerouac

Don't be discouraged by failure. It's often the last key in the bunch that opens the lock.

When your dreams turn to dust, it's time to get out the vacuum cleaner.

You can give without loving, but you can never love without giving.

The
Wisdom
of Ages

For classical thinkers, whether historians, philosophers, writers or poets, wisdom was considered to be central to the evolution of civilized humanity. In particular, self-knowledge, summed up in the maxim 'Know thyself', was highly prized as the first step on the path to true wisdom … as you will find out here.

Wise men speak because they have something to say; fools because they have to say something. *Plato*

Those who know are wise; those who know themselves are enlightened. *Lao Tzu*

The function of wisdom is to discriminate between good and evil. *Cicero*

Even a fool, when he holdeth his peace, is counted wise: and he that shutteth his lips is esteemed a man of understanding. *Proverbs 17.28*

To be fond of learning is near to wisdom. *Confucius*

Wisdom is the supreme part of happiness.

Sophocles

Wise men must seek to understand the truth of their own nature.
The Bhagavad Gita

It is the nature of the wise to resist pleasures, but the foolish to be a slave to them. *Epictetus*

Cleverness is not wisdom.

Euripides

From the errors of others, a wise man corrects his own.

Publilius Syrus

No man was ever wise by chance.
Seneca

**Nobody can give you
wiser advice than yourself.**

Cicero

Look to this day!
For it is life, the very life of life.
In its brief course
Lie all the verities and realities of your existence:
    The bliss of growth,
    The glory of action,
    The splendour of achievement,
For yesterday is but a dream
And tomorrow is just a vision,
And today well lived makes every yesterday a
    dream of happiness
And every tomorrow a vision of hope.
Look well, therefore to this day!
Such is the salutation to the dawn.

Kalidasa

The only true wisdom is knowing that you know nothing. *Socrates*

The middle course is the best. *Cleobulus*

The first step in the acquisition of wisdom is silence; the second, listening; the third, memory; the fourth, practice; and the fifth, teaching others. *Solomon Ibn Gabirol*

Wonder is the beginning of wisdom.
Socrates

The sky changes, not the soul,
for whom travels the sea.
Horace

Wisdom, compassion, and courage, are the three universally recognized moral qualities of men.

Confucius

I don't need a friend who nods when I nod, and who changes when I change. My shadow does that much better.

Plutarch

Wise kings have wise counsellors; and he must be a wise man himself who is capable of recognizing one.
Diogenes

A fool is wise in his own eyes.

King Solomon

He whose wisdom exceeds his works, to what may he be likened? To a tree whose branches are numerous but whose roots are few. The wind comes along and it uproots it, and sweeps it down. *The Talmud*

Wisdom outweighs any wealth. *Sophocles*

Nature and wisdom never are at strife. *Plutarch*

A wise man learns by the mistakes of others, a fool by his own.

Latin proverb

By associating with wise people, you will become wise yourself.
Menander

True wisdom is less presuming than folly. The wise man doubteth often, and changeth his mind; the fool is obstinate, and doubteth not; he knoweth all things but his own ignorance. *Akhenaton*

The highest form of wisdom is kindness.

The Talmud

How prone to doubt, how cautious are the wise! *Homer*

Be kind, for everyone you meet is fighting a hard battle. *Seneca*

Wisdom is the conqueror of fortune. *Juvenal*

Perfect wisdom has four parts: Wisdom, the principle of doing things aright; justice the principle of doing things equally in public and in private; fortitude, the principle of not fleeing danger, but meeting it; and temperance, the principle of subduing desires and living moderately. *Plato*

Know thyself.

Inscription at the
Temple of Apollo, Delphi

By three methods we may learn wisdom; first, by reflection, which is noblest; second, by imitation, which is easiest; and third, by experience, which is bitterest. *Confucius*

That is true wisdom, to know how to change one's mind when occasion demands it.
Terence

Philosophy, rightly defined, is simply the love of wisdom.
Cicero

To walk safely through the maze of human life, one needs the light of wisdom and the guidance of virtue. **Buddha**

Through suffering comes wisdom. *Aeschylus*

Silence at the proper season is wisdom, and better than any speech. *Plutarch*

Great doubts, deep wisdom; small doubts, little wisdom.
Chinese proverb

Where fear is present, wisdom cannot be. *Lactantius*

It is fortune, not wisdom, that rules man's life. *Cicero*

Do not be frightened or bewildered by the luminous, brilliant, very sharp and clear blue light of supreme wisdom, for it is the light-ray of the Buddha.

Tibetan Book of the Dead

Knowledge without justice should be called cunning rather than wisdom. *Plato*

You cannot step into the same river twice, for fresh waters are ever flowing in upon you. *Heraclitus*

In the country of the blind, the one-eyed man is king.

Erasmus

The lips of the wise are as the doors of a cabinet; no sooner are they opened but treasures are poured out before thee.

Akhenaton

In youth and beauty, wisdom is but rare.
Homer

Man is the measure of all things; of things that are, that they are; and of things that are not, that they are not. *Protagoras*

If you want to improve, be content to be thought foolish and stupid.
Epictetus

The pine stays green in winter, as does wisdom in hardship.

Chinese proverb

To make no mistakes is not in the power of man; but from their errors and mistakes the wise and good learn wisdom for the future.
Plutarch

The unexamined life is not worth living.
Socrates

The words of the wise are like cattle prods – painful but helpful. Their collected sayings are like a nail-studded stick with which a shepherd drives the sheep. *Ecclesiastes*

Experience is the mother of wisdom.

Chinese proverb

I often regret that I have spoken; never that I have been silent. **Publilius Syrus**

Sometimes even to live is an act of courage.
Seneca

It is not death that a man should fear, but he should fear never beginning to live.
Marcus Aurelius

Give me but one firm spot on which to stand, and I will move the earth. **Archimedes**

Nil desperandum.
Never despair.
Horace

To be satisfied with a little, is the greatest wisdom; and he that increaseth his riches, increaseth his cares; but a contented mind is a hidden treasure, and trouble findeth it not.

Akhenaton

This is the very perfection of a man, to find his imperfections.
Saint Augustine

How to be Wise

It is not easy to be wise. For most people, it's a life's work, and one that is never entirely fulfilled. However calm, sensible, and balanced we think we become as we grow older, there are always moments when we lose our heads. In this section, you'll find some thoughts about how to deal with these moments when they happen, and how to move forward with courage and determination.

The wisest words are often the simplest and most direct.

Colours fade, temples crumble, empires fall, but wise words endure.

Edward Thorndike

When you feel angry, try saying what you have to say without using harsh words or raising your voice. You'll be surprised how much better people will react.

Wherever you go, go with all your heart.

Confucius

Don't be too harsh on yourself. Be a wise friend instead.

Righteous anger has its place, but it must be used sparingly, for its value decreases every time you use it.

Love and work are the cornerstones of our humanness. *Freud*

The reckless person spends money as it comes in. The wise person saves for a rainy day. The fool refuses to dip into his hoard even when that rainy day comes.

Fall down seven times; stand up eight.

Chinese proverb

One of the greatest gifts of wisdom is knowing when to speak and when to remain silent.

If you can't think of anything good to say, don't say anything.

Nobody can do better than their very best.

Neither a borrower nor a lender be; for loan oft loseth both itself and friend. *William Shakespeare*

Don't try to defy age. If you do, you'll be fighting a losing battle.

In a situation of conflict, wisdom is often a question of identifying people's needs and allowing each side to voice them.

Instead of envying other people's wealth and happiness, count your own blessings. You may find they add up to more than you imagined.

Be who you are and say what you feel, because those who mind don't matter, and those who matter don't mind.

Dr Seuss

Wisdom is giving and receiving empathy, as well as being open and honest.

You can only fail if you give up.

The songbird is neither wise nor foolish. It simply sings.

Follow your inner moonlight; don't hide the madness.

Allen Ginsberg

Necessity is the mother of invention.

Learn to love others despite their faults; and they will learn to love you back.

Resilience is not something we are born with. It is something we have to build, by taking time to cultivate a supportive network of family and friends – people that we can go to in times of need.

Don't find fault. Find a remedy.

Henry Ford

Knowing when and how to ask for help is part of true wisdom.

Be a realistic optimist: understand that bad things can happen, but meet the challenges of life, hoping for a positive outcome.

If you lose your temper, you've lost the battle.

Better to have a few good friends than many false ones.

Those who have survived serious illness sometimes experience it as a 'wake-up call', encouraging them to focus on priorities, and to live life to the full.

Before you can understand other people, you must understand yourself.

Shared sorrow can bring us closer to those we love.

Be careful of the words you say
Keep them short and sweet
You never know, from day to day,
Which ones you'll have to eat.

Be yourself – nobody else can be better at it than you!

March to the beat of your own drum.

Every truth passes through three stages before it is recognized.
In the first, it is ridiculed; in the second, it is opposed; and in the third, it is regarded as self-evident.

Arthur Schopenhauer

If you make a mistake, have the courage to own up to it.

Believe in miracles …
but don't rely on them!

It's no good telling people you
are wise. You have to show
them through your actions.

Friendship is love without his wings!
Lord Byron

Life's problems wouldn't be called 'hurdles' if there was no way to get over them.

Love may mean nothing in tennis, but it means everything in life.

The happiest of all lives is a busy solitude.
Voltaire

No matter how long the winter, spring is sure to follow.

Don't wish you could go back and make a new start. Start from where you are, and make a new ending.

Put your future in good hands – your own.

Sometimes love blinds us. Sometimes it opens our eyes.

Words without thoughts never to heaven go.

William Shakespeare

There are many things you think you can't do – until you do them!

Autumn is a second spring when every leaf is in flower.

Albert Camus

When we cannot get what we love, we must love what is in our reach.

Slowing down is seldom a waste of time. It can actually be a way of saving, and savouring, time.

Play the music, not the instrument.

Advice is what we ask for when we know the answer but wished we didn't.

Erica Jong

It is always wise to be kind. Even if your kindness is not returned, others will perhaps learn something from your behaviour.

The true sign of wisdom is continual cheerfulness.

I've failed over and over again in my life. And that is why I succeed. *Michael Jordan*

Sitting quietly, doing nothing, spring comes, and the grass grows by itself. *Zen proverb*

It's good to be important, but it's more important to be good.

The best portion of a
 good man's life – his little,
nameless, unremembered
acts of kindness.

William Wordsworth

**Treat everyone you
meet with courtesy – not
because they are nice,
but because you are.**

Being a parent is the one job where, if you're successful, you end up unemployed.

If the young knew and the old could, there is nothing that couldn't be done.

**It is not heard at all,
but you are the music
While the music lasts.**

T. S. Eliot

Wisdom comes from listening, not speaking.

The wise person is able not only to discern right from wrong, and truth from delusion, but to act on what he finds.

In giving advice, seek to help, not to please, your friend.
Solon

Wisdom lies not in following rules, but in making them.

I always pass on good advice. It's the only thing to do with it. It is never any use to oneself. *Oscar Wilde*

In order to get things done, we need routines. But we also need to know when to break our routines, so that we can respond to the moment.

Gossip and lies go hand in hand.

We often fail in our struggle to be wise, but if we succeed, the rewards are great: inner peace, contentment, and a sound belief in our own judgement.

Are we not formed, as notes of music are
For one another, though dissimilar?
Percy Bysshe Shelley

Live compassionately.
Help others to grow.

If you would be a seeker
after truth, you must learn to
doubt everything.
Descartes

Wisdom lies in seeing what needs to be done, without being blinded by one's own personal desires, fears, likes, and dislikes.

Children may not be wise, but they are often more truthful than the adults around them.

Good advice is beyond price.

You don't really understand human nature unless you know why a child on a merry-go-round will wave at his parents every time around – and why his parents will always wave back. *William D. Tammeus*

Simplicity is the seal of truth.

Wisdom is: understanding; action; thought; knowledge; experience; compassion; anticipation; prudence; discernment; and, most of all, love.

Many of life's failures are people who did not realize how close they were to success when they gave up.

Thomas Edison

The universe is a giant, complex system. Remember that you are a tiny part of it, not the centre of it.

Wisdom is the ability to see things from the point of view of the whole.

There is no psychiatrist in the world like a puppy licking your face.

Bernard Williams

The wise are not the possessors of wisdom, but the lovers of wisdom.

Wisdom is a virtue widely treasured but seldom explained.

I believe that all wisdom consists in caring immensely for a few right things, and not caring a straw about the rest.

John Buchan

As an inborn trait, wisdom is a rare quality; as a result of experience, it is more common.

What makes us wise? First, that we have wide knowledge and experience. Second, that we know how to live well. Third, that we can teach others by our own example.

If you surrender to the wind, you can ride it.

Toni Morrison

A wise friend is someone who understands you better than you understand yourself.

A good book is like a secluded garden carried in the pocket.
Chinese proverb

One generation plants the trees; the next get the shade.

Keep a green tree in your heart, and perhaps a songbird will find it.

Wisdom is the quality that keeps you from getting into situations where you need it.
Doug Larson

More than we use is more than we need.

We know that time changes everything, so why are we always so surprised when change comes?

If you fill your days with busy activity and strict routine, your life will go by very fast. To slow it down, take time out now and then …

Unable are the loved to die.
For love is immortality. *Emily Dickinson*

True wisdom lies in having the ability to see others as they are, not as you would like them to be.

Sometimes it's better to be kind than to be truthful.

If you're going through hell, keep going.
Winston Churchill

When you lose, don't lose the lesson.

The future lies before you
Like paths of pure white snow.
Be careful how you tread it
For every step will show.

We can never truly reach our goal, since when we arrive at it, we will immediately see another further ahead.

Nature has much to teach us about wisdom, if we can only observe it: whether in the passing of the seasons, or the interconnectedness of animal and plant life.

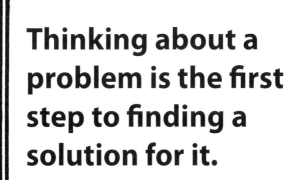

Thinking about a problem is the first step to finding a solution for it.

On the mountains of truth you can never climb in vain; either you will reach a point higher up today, or you will be training your powers so that you will be able to climb higher tomorrow. *Friedrich Nietzsche*

Before others can love us, we need to learn to love ourselves.

Laughter is good for you. And you can't overdose on it!

The small truth has words that are clear; the great truth has great silence.

Rabindranath Tagore

Being afraid to make mistakes is one of the biggest mistakes you can make.

Ask questions from the heart and you will be answered from the heart.

Native American proverb

There is a loftier ambition than merely to stand high in the world. It is to stoop down and lift mankind a little higher.
Henry Van Dyke

Better to retreat into solitude than to surround yourself with false friends.

Keep your eyes on the stars, and your feet on the ground.

Theodore Roosevelt

Don't postpone joy until you have learned all your lessons. Joy is your lesson.

Alan Cohen

If we seek wisdom, we may find it by looking at the infinity of the ocean, the grandeur of the sky, the twinkling of the stars at night, or a single autumn leaf falling to the ground.

We are always free to make choices, even if our circumstances may limit those choices.

The way you live your life should be a reflection of your core values.

If you don't get lost,
there's a chance you
may never be found.

The truly wise person is the one who knows how to deal with the disappointments of life, not just the successes.

Wisdom is a question of reflecting long and hard before you act.

True silence is the rest of the mind, and is to the spirit what sleep is to the body: nourishment and refreshment.

William Penn

Reaching our goals is not always as exciting as we expect. Sometimes, we may look back and realize we were happier when we were on our way up.

All men should strive to learn before they die What they are running from, and to, and why.

James Thurber

Having many choices in life does not always make people happy. In fact, it can make them miserable, worrying that they've made the wrong ones.

The Proverbs

Over the centuries, ordinary people from many cultures across the world have gathered together the collective advice of their communities – some humorous, some poetic – in ancient proverbs and sayings. In many cases we do not know where these aphorisms come from; but, direct and pithy as they are, we can guess that they represent the distilled wisdom of generations.

Time and tide wait for no man.

He that knows little often repeats it.

Give me a fish, I have the day's food. Teach me how to fish, I have every day's food.

Good fences make good neighbours.

Learn to walk before you try to run.

A heart that loves is always young.

Out of sight, out of mind.

He travels fastest who travels alone.

The road to hell is paved with good intentions.

Old sins cast long shadows.

More haste, less speed.

A still tongue makes a wise head.

A trouble shared is a trouble halved.

Believe nothing of what you hear, and only half of what you see.

You can lead a horse to water but you can't make him drink.

Do not judge your neighbour till you walk two moons in his moccasins.

Eat to live, do not live to eat.

The devil finds work for idle hands.

A bird in the hand is worth two in the bush.

Every beetle is beautiful in the eyes of its mother.

All good things come to an end.

Don't count your chickens before they're hatched.

When the blind lead the blind, both will fall in the ditch.

Empty vessels make the most sound.

Even an eagle cannot soar higher than the stars.

A fool and his money are soon parted.

Young men think old men to be fools; old men know young men to be so.

Yesterday is ashes, tomorrow wood. Only today does the fire burn brightly.

One man's meat is another man's poison.

You can't judge a book by looking at the cover.

The best wine comes from an old cask.

Wisdom and virtue are like the two wheels of a cart.

Only a fool is scornful of the commonplace.

You can't make an omelette without breaking eggs.

Least said, soonest mended.

One does not love if one does not accept from others.

What's sauce for the goose is sauce for the gander.

Don't depend on someone else if you can be your own master.

You reap what you sow.

The sky is open to those who have wings.

Put out a fire while it is still small.

When a father gives to his son, both laugh; when a son gives to his father, both cry.

A friend is the greatest treasure in life.

A habit does not make a monk.

Good health is worth more than the greatest wealth.

Practice makes perfect.

History is the tutor of life.

Better to die fighting, than live fleeing.

Rome wasn't built in a day.

Time flees, eternity dwells.

Drink is the curse of the land. It makes you fight with your neighbour. It makes you shoot at your landlord. It makes you miss him.

A mother understands what a child does not say.

There's no smoke without fire.

One swallow doesn't make a summer.

He conquers who conquers himself.

**Listen to the voice of nature,
for it holds treasure for you.**

A leopard
cannot change
its spots.

Let not the sun go down upon your wrath.

It is easy to be brave from a distance.

Pride goes before destruction, and a haughty spirit before stumbling.

Everyone is kneaded out of the same dough but not baked in the same oven.

For a good appetite, there is no hard bread.

He who wakes early meets a golden day.

The grass is always greener on the other side.

If you marry a monkey for his wealth, the money goes, and the monkey remains.

The old horse in the stable still yearns to run a thousand miles.

The more you give, the more good things come to you.

Sound
Advice

Wisdom is not always profound and mysterious. It can also be practical, sensible, and down to earth. Here, we look at the whole range of thoughts, ideas, and lessons that constitute sound advice from the wise.

Where one is wise, two are happy.

Each person writes their own story as he or she goes through life. Every day is a new paragraph, a new page, a new chapter, or even a whole new book.

Worry never robs tomorrow of its sorrow; it only saps today of its joy.

Leo Buscaglia

When life hands you a lemon … make lemonade.

You are not unique. Another human being, at some time or place, will have gone through the same roller-coaster experiences, of pain and joy, despair and hope, that you do. It's called living.

Fortune favours the bold, but abandons the timid. *Latin proverb*

There are two refuges from the miseries of life: music and cats.
Albert Schweitzer

You only have one life here on earth – make the most of it.

Sometimes a tough situation can turn out to be a gift, bringing forth love, courage, strength, and kindness from oneself and others that, hitherto, has been hidden.

Knowledge of what is possible
is the beginning of happiness.

George Santayana

**Empathy is not something we
should occasionally show; it should
be a constant frame of mind,
characterized by openness and
sensitivity to the feelings of others.**

What comes from the heart, goes to the heart.
Samuel Taylor Coleridge

It's easy to get angry; much harder to explain politely what you need, why your needs have not been met, and how they could be met in the future.

The one who wills is the one who can.

Regret for wasted time is more wasted time.

Mason Cooley

What should we wish for our children? That they should be happy? Perhaps, but also that they should be themselves, and follow their own path, wherever it may lead them.

Gratitude is the best attitude.

Fear has its place as a rational response to danger, but it should never be a general presentiment that things will go wrong.

No road is long with good company.

Turkish proverb

Respect begins with oneself.

Everyone deceives themselves
at times; but only the wise know
when, and why, they are doing so,
and are able to halt the process.

Hem your blessings with gratitude, so that they won't unravel.

If you can't explain it simply, you don't understand it well enough.

Albert Einstein

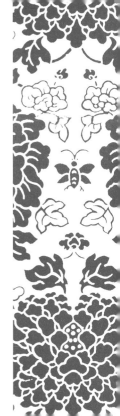

Memories are precious reminders of our past, but they should never become more important to us than the present, or the future.

The curious paradox is that when I accept myself just as I am, then I can change. *Carl Rogers*

**Life is an adventure –
don't be too busy to live it.**

Complaining often tells people more about the negative way you deal with life than how bad your circumstances really are.

When you are content to be simply yourself, and don't compare or compete, everybody will respect you. *Lao Tzu*

Gratitude turns a simple meal into a banquet fit for kings.

Don't criticize yourself for failing, only for not trying in the first place.

To live content with small means; to seek elegance rather than luxury, and refinement rather than fashion; to be worthy, not respectable, and wealthy, not rich; to listen to stars and birds, babes and sages, with open heart; to study hard; to think quietly, act frankly, talk gently, await occasions, hurry never; in a word, to let the spiritual, unbidden and unconscious, grow up through the common – this is my symphony.

William Ellery Channing

'Now' is the watchword of the wise.

If you're generous, kind, and polite, don't necessarily expect others to follow suit. It may take them a while to learn from your example.

Earning money is like digging with a needle; spending it is like throwing water into sand.

Japanese proverb

By others' faults the wise correct their own.

The best path to wisdom is an enquiring mind; the best guide, a humble spirit.

One ought, every day at least, to hear a little song, read a good poem, see a fine picture, and, if it were possible, to speak a few reasonable words.

Johann Wolfgang von Goethe

The mind, like the body, needs the daily discipline of exercise. If you don't use it regularly, you will lose the capacity to think in a focused way.

If it were not for hope, the heart would break.

Always keep an open mind. You may feel inclined to dismiss certain ideas straight away as wrong; but at least consider them carefully before you reject them.

The gardener must sometimes plant many seeds before a single flower grows.

There is a remedy for everything except death.

Try to find the beauty in the world around you; and to make it more beautiful, even in a small way.

The wise man looks for the best in others, rather than the worst.

If we could learn to like ourselves, even a little, maybe our cruelties and angers might melt away.

John Steinbeck

What will others have learned from you when you leave this world behind? Ask yourself that question, and if you can find no answer, start thinking about the way you are living your life.

Vision without action is a daydream. Action without vision is a nightmare.

Think of someone you love. What is it that you love about them? Could they say the same of you, or are your qualities different?

Worry not that no one knows of you; seek to be worth knowing.

Confucius

Not all of us are wise. Sometimes we love the foolishness in our friends and family – and even in ourselves. For it is foolishness that makes us human.

Even broken clocks are right twice a day.

**Don't seek for love.
Let love find you.
That way, you will fall,
without being pushed.**

Just because we can't change everything doesn't mean we shouldn't try to change anything.

Most people would rather die than think. Many do. *Bertrand Russell*

If you can leave the world knowing that you have brought an element of love, peace, joy, and wisdom into it, even in the smallest way, your life will have been well worth living.

A prophet is not without honour save in his own country. *The Bible*

The mark of an educated mind is the ability to entertain an idea without accepting it.
Aristotle

Days go by slowly, years quickly. This is the paradox of time, and one that we struggle to understand.

When people are bored, it is primarily with themselves.

Eric Hoffer

Ordinary life is largely made up of chores and routines. But if we try to do them with love, care, and concentration, they will begin to seem less dull.

I wish I could show you
when you are lonely or in
darkness the astonishing
light of your own being.

Hafiz

In teaching others,
we teach ourselves.